Sam's
New Baby

For my grandchildren
Jan Godfrey

Especially for Sam
Jane Coulson

Sam's
New Baby

Jan Godfrey
Illustrated by Jane Coulson

Abingdon Press

It was a snowy day, but Sam and his friends were warm and cosy inside their classroom. They were busy looking through magnifying glasses.

"See if you can find out what happens when you look through the glass," said Sam's teacher.

They looked at the grainy pattern on their chairs, and the knitted pattern on their jumpers. Then they looked at Martha's hair. It was huge!

"Look at the patterns on your fingers," suggested Sam's teacher.

"They're not the same," said Sam as he and Robert held their fingers under the glass.

"Everyone's fingerprints are different," said Sam's teacher.

She poured some white paint into a saucer, and gave everyone a piece of black paper.

Sam made some finger prints, and then he turned them into a little person.

"I've made a finger baby!" said Sam. He looked through the magnifying glass again, and the finger baby grew bigger.

"My mom's going to have a baby soon," said Sam. "It's growing inside her and my grandma's come to stay."

"That's great, Sam," smiled his teacher. "Your new baby's going to be very special."

"I'm special," said Kate. "I've got three brothers and I'm the only girl."

"I'm special," said Ben. "I'm adopted. My mom and dad CHOSE me out of lots of other babies."

"I'm special," said Lara. "I haven't got any brothers or sisters."

"We're special," said Rebecca and Robert. "There were two of us born at once. We're twins."

Sam didn't say anything. He looked at everyone through his magnifying glass. He wasn't sure if he was special or not. He hoped he was.

Dad and Grandma fetched Sam from school
that day. They trudged home together
through the falling snow. Sam tried to catch a
snowflake so he could look at it under his
magnifying glass at home.

"Am I special?" asked Sam.

"Of course you are," said Dad.

"You're my special Sam," said Grandma.

"I made a finger baby today," Sam told Mom and Dad at bedtime. He felt for his magnifying glass under his pillow. "Will our baby be a boy or a girl?"

"We'll have to wait and see," said Dad.

Sam held the glass up to Mom's tummy.

"James or Jessica? What do you think?" laughed Mom.

"I don't know,' said Sam, "I can't see anything."

"God can!" said Dad. "That's God's secret."

"Does God know already?" asked Sam.

"God knows everything," said Mom. "God knows us when we are growing inside our mommies. God even knows our names."

"Does God know our fingerprints?" asked Sam, looking at his fingers once more.

"God chose the pattern!" laughed Dad.

"Wow!" said Sam. "But there are so many. How does God know?"

"God just does!" said Mom, tucking him into bed.

That night, while the stars shone and the snow sparkled, Sam's new baby was born.

"Wake up, Sam!" came Dad's voice. "It's morning and you've got a new little... SISTER!"

"My new baby's been born," Sam told his
teacher. "She's called Jessica and she's
special."

And Sam's teacher said, "She must be
VERY special. You're her big brother!"

"My new baby's been born," Sam told the postman when he came with a pile of cards. "She's called Jessica and she's special."

And the postman said, "She must be VERY special. Look at all those cards!"

Some of Sam's aunts and uncles came to visit.
They took it in turns to cuddle Jessica and
play snowballs with Sam.

But Mom was tired, and Dad was busy cooking meals and making tea and washing baby clothes. The house felt very busy and noisy and topsy-turvy. Sam began to feel disappointed.

He went to sit on Grandma's lap.

"Hello, Sam," she said. "Do you want to play in the snow? Or shall I read you a story?"

"I don't know," mumbled Sam. He felt sad. There were too many people. They got in the way. Nothing felt the same.

"I've got a good idea!" said Grandma suddenly. "I'll take all the grown-ups out for a walk, while you stay here with Mom and Dad and Jessica."

"OK," said Sam. He wasn't sure whether it was a good idea or not.

"I think you'll need your magnifying glass," said Grandma as she put on her boots.

"Come and help me give Jessica a bath," said
Mom.
    Mom and Dad bathed Jessica.

Dad wrapped Jessica in a towel.
"Would you like to hold her, Sam?" asked Dad.
Sam held Jessica very, very carefully on his lap.

Sam looked at Jessica through his magnifying glass.

He looked at her face. She had tiny milk spots. He looked at her head, and saw her wispy hair. He looked at her eyes and tried to count her tiny little eyelashes.

Cautiously he put his finger into hers, and saw the brand new patterns on her fingers. Sam thought about God's secret. Jessica curled her tiny new fingers round Sam's finger and held onto it tightly.

Sam looked at his new baby sister.

"She's holding my finger!" said Sam in surprise. "She knows me!"

"She's a real finger baby," said Dad.

"She's the best," said Sam happily. "She is special."

"And so are you," said Mom and Dad together, giving him a hug. "Our own special Sam."

Published in the United States of America by
Abingdon Press
201 Eighth Avenue South
PO Box 801
Nashville, TN 37202–0801

ISBN 0-687-09570-0

First edition 1998

Printed and bound in Singapore